Stargazing
UNDER THE SUN
Naveesa Zaheer

IBSN: 1723003980
IBSN-13: 978-1723003981

Dedication

With special regards to my family
and in tribute to Madiha Wasi.
| 27 – 02 – 2017 |

contents:

The hardest battle is the one that you fight with yourself – it is the one where your heart battles your mind, and there is a war of logic and ethics. On Monday 27th February 2017, 21:56pm, that war had started within me. My heart was placed in the witness box, while my mind desperately attempted to bail it out. My best friend had passed away, six months after confronting me about her depression. Without a doubt, the cause of her death was natural, but undoubtedly her mental health had played its part too. Yet, it wasn't what she had told me about her depression that threw me off; rather, it was her jokingly made invitation to me to her funeral, a day before her death, that had dragged me into this courtroom. My heart would mock my mind – you've helped people out before, how could you fail on her? Equally, my mind would mock my heart – why did not feel the scrapes of her requests? My mind would tell me – there was nothing I could have done; while my heart would remind me – she left believing that she wasn't good enough.

This war in its description is unexplainable – no one could help me out, other than myself. From having it all together, I lost it all – it had become my sharpest fall. From one of the brightest students who'd just secured themselves a seat in one of the world's most prestigious university, I'd fallen – rock bottom.

I was merely a lost traveller whose companion found their destination in the middle of what should have been our journey. It felt as if I'd been dropped from the clouds – into the sea – with a heart that kept telling me I had failed, and a mind that told me to breathe. My younger self kept telling me to get up, while the reflection in the mirror kept shaking her head at me.

Interestingly, everything from that moment worked the opposite way. I didn't secure any of my then 'dream' internships. Many people stopped asking of me when they found out I was under heavy rain. All of a sudden, I was in the middle of the sea, and I could see my dreams drifting away from me. I didn't understand, I had prayed to reach to this stage, so why was it all falling out of place? I would open the window every day and just stare into the sky like a wilted flower complaining to the sun of the rain. There was so much to say, yet there was no way of expression but silence. I read that struggles are blessings in disguise, yet I didn't understand how I would gain in this loss. I read that if one has good intentions, the doors for them are opened. I would think to myself – surely, God was aware of my bigger dream – He must know that I had always wished to make my parents proud and had aspired to open schools for the poor – so why was it, that everything was falling apart now that I was so close to achieving what I had put my mind to?

The world is correct to say that bad times teach you, what good times never could. *The beauty of success is the struggle to achieve.* This fall had certainly changed my perception and taught me to rise under the rain – not after it. I used to think I needed a status to pursue my intentions, but this phase taught me that one's intentions make their status. Surely, He wasn't ignoring me – He was leading me a different way, where He blessed me with the opportunity to change mindsets and lives. The beauty of this route was helping people as I helped myself – not lending a hand once I'd gotten up.

Yet getting to this stage I realised, to write what is right is not easy. People told me, write some lines of poetry on love, it'll take you places – add 'self' at the start of love and your poetry will quiver among the rest. I do not agree – I write what I stand for, and I say what society and culture silences. It is that, this world puts gender equality in pay, before gender equality in justice – just as a man cannot stand in court and point at a woman, a girl cannot refuse marriage to a man twice her age in exchange for a chance to educate herself. Honour killing still exists, rape allegations are a stain on the woman, young girls grow up as victims. Culture turns away at the mention of depression, love is wrongly defined as infatuation, comparison is equally weighted in the air as oxygen. I took the risk and wrote against the trend – I wrote to remind others, of what is written in the clouds – *a soul is never burdened beyond its capability to bear – it is never tested greater than the strength it holds to overcome.*

This world is unjust, yet in its imbalance, there is betterment. Everything has end, yet it is often mistaken that storms only end once one has reached their end – that is wrong. Sometimes, it happens that one focuses so much on what is seen, existence is overlooked – it is as if, memory deceives, and what is remembered are misfortunes, while miracles are forgotten. It is, that one knows of the body they roam in, compares it to the bodies that roam around them, but forget of the soul that roams within. As if, the focus is so much on the clouds that the stars that sit amongst the sun are forgotten of. In its possible impossibility, it is as such – *stargazing under the sun.*

stargazing under the sun

a note for

you

a reminder to begin with,
to remember when you feel
everything is ending.

time is not constant –
it is, that it may be winter
in your home

> while it is summer in your
> neighbour's

while the uncertainty of
autumn

> and impatience of spring
> is sitting elsewhere.

the seed of a tree that sits
so comfortability
in one's palm
is destined to outgrow the one
who plants it.
often, impossibility is defined
by logic –
but time does not work that way.
if you dream,
have the courage to aspire –
do what you can
in honesty,
with love,
and leave the rest on time.
the winds dance to your
intentions –
if the intentions are pure,
be ready to go head on
in the war to acquire.

if you are struggling,
keep fighting.

*fate is
unpredictable*

if you fall,
stand up again.
never give up
assuming
it will not happen.
*time cannot
resurrect you
when everything is
waiting to fall
in place.*

never decide for yourself
that this world doesn't need you
or your prayers
shatter against the sky.
*fate has woven itself
in your palm –*
let it lead you.
don't cut it to its end,
when it is reading you
the middle.

stargazing under the sun

a note for your

your body is your soul's home
– that is all.

your body is not a monument,
nor is this world a museum –
it is not your job to cater
your looks
to their expectations.
your body is your soul's home –
that is all.
time does not permit you
to keep it in its form.
it is bound to decay,
with time and with age.
yet this world keeps telling you
to preserve what won't last and,
in its process,
damage what is to remain.

perfection is subjective –
cocooned in impossibility,
(unachievable)
for it demands that one
must satisfy seven billion
opinions.
that is not incapability,
that is not worthlessness,
that is not the fault of your skin,
that is not the fault of your height,
that is not the fault of your weight,
that is not your fault.
at its simplest,
it is an undisputed impossibility
for anyone.

and they discriminate against
colour and culture –
skin texture.
age and height –
the thickness of your thighs.
it is as if so,
the soul *decays*
and the body *escapes*.

wounds stitched close
(in fear)
with the string
of anxiety,
do not heal.
they are merely forced
into silence,
and awoken by
the memories that graze them.
it becomes a necessary
necessity to leave them
under the sun –
to heal.
> *(salt dropped on scars*
> *does not sting the new skin)*

do not beg for acceptance
from wondering eyes,
and a mind that plays the tune
of indecisiveness.
they will make you believe that
change *for you*
is necessary,
while their eyes will convince them
that change *from you*
to another
is necessary.
you will lose trying to earn
their acceptance.
(yet you would earn more
if you chased self-acceptance)

your *self-worth* will smile,
when you let go of those
who brushed you
out of their heart
during spring,
and make room for nature
that awaits to make
its home in you.
your *self-esteem* will glow,
when you close the door on those
who demand for you to wear on
expectations
as your skin.
the love that you have
for yourself
will grow,
when you accept yourself,
and reject all those who refuse
to accept you.
> *(it is you before them,*
> *not them before you)*

never forget where you came from,
you are nothing without
your roots.
a rose plucked from its head
can grow again,
but pulled from its roots,
it is nothing
but a memory of what
it used to be.

> *(accomplishments and growth do not*
> *encourage arrogance –*
> *what has grown, was once young)*

never let people tell you
how much you can grow.
there are those who judge
by the *size* of the seed,
and others who merely
glance upon the soil.
the ones who judge growth
by comparison
always fail in their accuracy.
turn towards nature
and it will tell you,
it grew from the smallest.
admire yourself in the mirror –
your body,
your bones,
the veins that dance within you,
the organs vigorously working,
your heart that is feeling –
they will tell you.
> *miracles and magic dismiss*
> *size and logic.*

you are work
in progress.
like a half-completed portrait,
sitting on a painter's canvas.
like a caterpillar
cocooned,
waiting to break open.
like the bud of a rose,
ready to blossom.
there is a difference
between
being incomplete
and being a
masterpiece in progress.

a sword laced in honey,
will not make you bleed
any less.
just as poison,
with a teaspoon of sugar,
does not change what it is.
if they graze you *once*,
they can cut you *twice*,
and stab you *thrice*.
it is better for you,
to cry in their remembrance
(for a while),
than it is for you to bleed
in the remembrance of yourself
(forever).

you are art.
painted in scars,
a tale of wars,
a masterpiece made
in chaos.
that is the beauty
of you,
that you mistakenly
brush off
as mistakes,
regrets,
and imperfections.

> *you are art. at your best*
> *and at your worst.*
> *you are art.*

put yourself first –
let your soul breathe,
let your mind rest,
let your heart dance to
the rhythm of its beat.
for once,
do not force your soul
to question its home.
for once,
do not beg your heart
to accept wonderers
who knock for love
from door to door.
for once,
put yourself first and
let nature make its home in you.

your worth is not defined
by what others think of you.
your worth is defined by
what *you* think of yourself.
it is not shown by what others
think you deserve,
it is shown by what *you*
are willing to accept.
it is not when they regret
losing you,
it is when *you* regret
trading your light
for their darkness.

> *(your worth is nothing to do with*
> *them, and everything to do with you*)

allow hope to dance
within your veins,
and step away from those
who graze knives against
your skin.
there is something so unique
about the scent of hope –
that makes the nonbelievers
want to believe,
and makes the ones crawling
want to run.
there is something so beautiful
about hope,
that revives lost faith,
and makes people want to dance
under the rain.
> *(it is as if, hope is a remedy,*
> *and faith is a cure)*

respect yourself enough,
to walk away from people
who make you feel
uncomfortable
in your own skin.
when your heart is saddened
by what it hears about its home,
walk those wonderers
out of the gates
you once let them through.
remind yourself –
repeat it again,
and again –
you don't need them.
you don't need the ones
who make you feel uncomfortable
in your own home.

self-love is not looking in the mirror
and telling yourself
you look better than yesterday.
self-love is looking your worth
in the eye
and apologising
for pulling at your skin –
ashamed by what people
would think.
there is a crucial difference,
between increasing the standards,
of beauty,
and increasing the standards
of what you deserve.

never dress yourself in the
'ideal' characteristics
that unfaithful lovers will
tell you about.
your body was not made,
for it be toyed
on the name of expectations.
your beauty relies on
your soul's comfortability
to make home in you,
not for others to use you.
      be you
      as you please –
      not as they wish.

forgive your body,
for dismissing perfection
as unnecessary,
and moulding with
uniqueness.
forgive your body,
for dismissing expectations,
and aspiring to define you.
forgive your body,
for dismissing comparison
and only thinking about you.
forgive your body,
and let those go
who sing bittersweet poetry
to your body demanding change.
> *(point such people to the door,*
> *your worth is undisputedly*
> *highly staked)*

stargazing under the sun

a note for your

heart

it beats for you, not for them
– don't forget.

cracks in concrete
give way to growth –
colour blossoming
from emptiness,
hope overriding
the suppressed.
so why are you so fearful,
of the cracks
in your beating heart –
how is it,
that the cracks in your heart
will not be filled with daisies,
when the living can grow
between that –
which does not live.

do not cocoon yourself
in a degrading relationship
because of your fear
of being exposed to new air.
your strength
is nature's way of reminding you
that you have your own wings
to fly
to better destinations,
than to curl up and live
in suffocation.

let go of relationships
that no longer sing
the melodies of the sun.
the ones who have promised
their perception
to negativity
will make you believe that
the rain is made to
suffocate your roots –
while they smoke fear
into your airways,
and make you exhale
all your hope.
let go of such people –
who focus on the dark
instead of the stars,
and the clouds instead
of the sun that wraps itself
within them.
> *(let the confused be confused,*
> *do not confuse your definitions*
> *for them)*

temporary people
disappear with the sun.
they are not
permanent residents –
merely summer travellers,
who enjoy the blanket of rays
that celebrate your happiness.
when it is time for you
to grow
and the rain
invites itself home,
they will leave you.
they are merely
summer travellers,
they do not know
winter's loyalty.

if they redefine beauty
and demand for you
to change –
there is no denying in saying,
that they can redefine love,
and demand for you to leave.
there is a crucial difference
between *redefining* love,
and seeing it in you,
and *recreating* you,
so you can define their love.

knock on the door of
self-love,
and it will never deny you.
it will not ask for
the ransom of your happiness,
for temporary comfort.
it will never demand for you
to undress from your characteristics,
and wear on society's ideals.
it is never too late
to be welcomed,
you'll never be sent back
from the entrance.
just try for once,
to go to the home of love.
-         *go home*

never invite guests
who tread on the mass of your
heart with dirty feet.
do not allow them
to enter you home,
when they have
unfinished business
from before.
never let them use you
to clean off old emotions,
only for them to wander off
to other destinations.
you are not a pitstop –
turn away such wonderers,
from the gates of your home.

stay away from people
who promise
each
word
to negativity –
the air will *suffocate*
and your lungs
will starve
of hope.
they promise you
internal damage
while they solemnly
smoke more words.

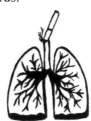

people deceive –
like the sun on a winter's morning,
that smiles a promise
it will not keep.
it is not incapability,
but rather unwillingness
(in human nature),
to wrap you in the rays of comfort
when the clouds are grey for you
(not them).
people deceive –
it is not what you deserve,
but it is an unfortunate
law of nature.

happiness will find you,
just like sadness did.
your troubles will leave you,
the right people will find you,
the rain will stop,
once you have grown enough,
to overcome what has
trapped you.
don't lose hope,
or compare yourself,
to the ones around you.
the clock is running,
but the time is different
for everyone.
> *(your story is yours, not theirs.*
> *time is leading you to your*
> *destination, and them to theirs)*

some people are like the clouds –
they seem close at sight,
but are far in reality.
they surround you,
they are constantly around you,
but when you reach out to them,
they are further than what
you can grab onto.
they are like the depths of the ocean,
you know of their existence,
yet to get to them is impossible.
if you chase people as such,
it will always be
you reaching out to them,
they will never reach out to you.
> *you will be left chasing*
> *what isn't even moving,*
> *simply as it is not*
> *written for your touch.*

forgive the ones
who tread in your heart
unwelcomed,
with flowers that mustered
the scent of beauty.
they were travellers
that lost their way –
merely searching for a museum
to admire,
they found home within the walls
of your heart
instead.
forgive them
for being so fearful,
of being wrapped within the magic
that runs within your veins.

it is strange –
the laws of this life.
heartbreak teaches you,
what love never could.
betrayal teaches you
not to lean on shadows,
not the sun.
loss awakens sentiments,
that presence never could.
until you haven't been thrown
mid-air,
you do not learn how to fly,
and until you haven't been pushed
into the sea,
you don't learn how to swim.
in its simplicity –

> *the one who hasn't suffered*
> *and endured,*
> *hasn't lived it all.*

it is impossible
to control the waves,
or guarantee the arrival
of a tide.
it is impossible
to predict the size –
how many there shall be
and how long they are to last.
it is impossible,
in the simplicity of their nature.
yet –
if you cannot control the waves,
you can learn how to swim.
you can learn how to glide,
instead of thrash.
you can learn how to waver
with their rhythm,
than panic out of balance.

    (there is a lot you can do
    for yourself – your faith
    must be stronger
    than your fear)

the hardest battle,
is the one that you fight with
yourself —
it is the one in which
your heart battles your mind,
and your ears battle your eyes.
the one in which
your younger self battles
the you of now,
in the chaos of what you are
to become.
it is the hardest battle
as you are fighting with the one
from which concealment
is impossible.

> *(it is you and you in war;*
> *and you and you*
> *who must settle peace)*

expectations from others
are promised disappointments,
sitting in a basket of uncertainty.
never expect from a heart
that does not beat for your soul,
and a mind that
(in its nature)
does not put you first.
if you wish for change,
happiness,
or love,
knock on the door of
your own heart.

your heart beats for you,
not for them –
don't forget.
do not tape your heart,
with expectations
of apologies and regrets
from those
who dirtied the mass
of its skin.
it does not need their apologies –
it needs yours.
it doesn't need their acceptance,
it needs yours.
> *it beats for you,*
> *not for them –*
> *don't forget.*

let it go –
open the windows of your heart
and let it breathe.
let your worries roam into nature,
and let your heart sing
with the winds into calmness.
your heart has spent too long
wrapped up in uncertainties –
let it breathe,
and allow nature to caress its wounds
until they bloom with flowers.
-    *you owe yourself that much.*

stargazing under the sun

a note for your

soul

self-acceptance and peace
go hand in hand.

you do not need validation –
just like the daisies do not ask
the roses if they should bloom;
and the dandelions do not ask
the daffodils if they can grow
next to them.
they all rise from the same soil
(at their own pace),
and greet the sun as equals.
validation is unnecessary
when you rise from the same soil,
but grow in your own uniqueness.

your relationship with
yourself
is like that between
a rose and its roots.
stability in winter
is guaranteed
when you *embrace*
every part of yourself.
the rain is necessary
for growth
when you learn to absorb
what it teaches.
the wind will not bother
you so much,
petals falling will not
hurt so much,
you will not break apart –
should you *embrace* your roots,
and *accept* them as the ones
that have kept you standing.

Every prayer flies past your sight,
weaving within the clouds,
to knock at the sky –
repeating your urge
and mimicking your desperation.
it is never unheard,
nor dismissed,
nor ignored.
the winds only sing one message –
if it is good for you,
it will come to you.

it is never,
that the sun does not rise.
it rises as it sets,
yet sometimes,
it lives within the clouds –
away from your sight.
and sometimes it sets earlier,
marrying you to the night.
while sometimes,
it stays longer,
as if it has drunk
the dark out of existence.
it rises as it sets,
greeting you every morning
as you rise from comfort.
it merely sets to its accord
to teach you
the principles of time.
(time teaches you
what books cannot)

instability is a promise
whispered in summer's breeze –
a weird imbalanced balance
that brings peace.
it is strange in its laws –
instability ensures certainty.
what is today will not be tomorrow.
yet this statement is only remembered
when the tides push you off
your haven.
that is to say –
when the excess of emotion is
in favour of you,
it is sincerely signed to commonality;
and when it is against you,
it is harshly promised to
mental torture.
yet to live in this imbalanced world,
you must make peace with instability,
when summer and winter
come to their peak –
unexpectedly.

roses bloom,
the wind dances,
the clouds separate –
welcoming the sun.
daisies cover the land,
birds sing as they float
wrapped within
the warmth.
butterflies break free
from old homes –
the grass colours itself
in vibrancy.
all in perfect rhythm,
in sync,
they hum,
greeting spring –
they are reborn.
　　　　('since when did winter
　　　　last forever', they laugh)

the scent of summer rain,
patters the rhythm of imbalance
(nature's favourite sound)
of two opposites coming
together as one.
it paints the sky in a beauty
unspeakable,
strengthening roots,
as nature blooms
to smile at the sun.
your heart sighs,
as your airways gulp the magic
of the perfect imbalance
that flavours the air with hope –
*much needed for the flowers
within you to grow.*

time is not your slave –
it will not do as you say,
or work as you please.
it will be,
that your neighbour will be
dancing with the rays of the sun,
while you sulk under the rain.
that is not to say that
happiness is not for you.
that is to remind you that your
destination is not there.
your roots need to be stronger,
you must grow taller,
you need to hold on –
just a little longer.
>   *(the rain will merely soak you,*
>   *it will never be enough*
>   *to drown you)*

if you are certain,
that after the moon,
the sun will return,
and after night,
day will return –
and if you are certain,
that nor rain,
nor snow
will fall at once forever –
then be certain,
you will not be sad forever.
(there is certainty,
in change)

sometimes,
it is good (for you)
to open the windows
and let the rain fall in.
sometimes,
it is better (for you)
to let the curtains dance
along with the humming
of the wind.
sometimes,
it becomes necessary
(for you)
to become one with nature
and feel,
rather than just see,
the magic.

do not sing
your perfect melody
over the rhythm less tunes
that you keep on playing.
the reality remains
unchanged
by noises of the dreams
you are too fearful pursue.

(fulfilment requires courage)

turbulences promise unsettled
certainties
that stability could never
guarantee.
that is to say,
that even in your loss
you are winning –
since what is lost,
is replaced,
and what is yours
is returned.
every prayer negotiates
for the better of you –
even struggles
are blessings in disguise.
              (what do you lose
              in loss, really?)

a rocky path with a destination,
is better,
than a smooth path
with a dead end.
walking on your own shaky legs,
is better,
than grabbing a firm hand
that intends
to push you down later.
a change in route and
separation from companions,
does not necessarily mean
there is a change in your
destination.

> *life has infinite ways*
> *of leading people*
> *to the same destination.*

inner peace is achieved
through forgiveness.
first of yourself
(from yesterday's naivety),
and then of those
who wronged you
(knowingly or unknowingly).
you cannot be at peace
if your mind is at war
with its decisions,
and your heart is at war
with its emotions.
make peace with yourself –
forgive yourself,
and forgive them.
(forgiveness is a law of peace)

you are not a shadow,
you are not yesterday,
you are not the autumn leaves,
that blew away with the wind.
you are
growing by day,
and recovering by night –
blooming,
as you rise.
it is the beauty of being human –
breaking tirelessly
and recreating yourself,
once again.

patience is an art.
it is belief in betterment,
during sadness.
it is telling the moon
about the sun,
and the clouds,
about the stars.
it is telling the rain
about your roots,
and the dirt
about your petals.
> *patience is knowing that*
> *nature does not lie about time.*

breathe in,
breathe out,
and let it go.
the winds will return
what is yours,
and nature will engulf
the rest.
never burden yourself,
or a hold a breath in –
do not torture yourself
that way.
let it go –
this is the basic law
of survival.

no amount of anxiety
can change the future,
just as your tears,
cannot erase what has been
inked in the past.
do not search too far
past the stars,
and never dig too deep
in the soil.
let it be,
let it go,
and do the best for you
today
(in honesty).
        time will bring
         all the rest in place.

stargazing under the sun

a note on what

society avoids

nature knows better about equality
and justice than humanity itself.

they say this world is progressing
yet a man cannot be a victim
of her
(barred by society),
and a girl cannot say no
to marriage
to a man her father's age
(muted by culture).
rape and assault roots from
the figure of women and girls
(as if they have written
biology's laws).
mental health is
overlooked, and casually
dismissed
(undermining human emotions).
certainly, it seems, this world
is in a state of progression
(a progressive state of regression).

when a rose is tugged out
from its roots,
or ripped apart from
its petals;
crushed by a step of
arrogance,
or a play of ego –
nature does not distinguish it
on any grounds.
it was a part of a valley
of its equals.
yet when this assault is
mirrored
on humanity,
justice must wait on society
and culture's quarrels
to decide how human one must be
for justice to be served.

> *what a shame –*
> *nature knows better about justice and*
> *equality than humanity itself.*

roses shrivel,
the sky falls to darkness –
thunderstorms rage
disagreement within the winds.
the walls of the court sulk,
unable to bear justice.
one thud –
and the birds are silenced,
the court is dismissed –
for lack of evidence,
on culture's plea of honour,
by the whiff of money,
or discrimination.
the miscarriage of justice,
is once again,
signed to paper.
    (within the clouds,
    it is written – you cannot
    carry more than your sins beyond them)

it is always the girl
and the woman
she is to become
that suffers.
it is *her* canvas,
that is blackened,
and *her* future
that is darkened.
it is she
who must stutter
in front of society,
and hide away
from culture.
never make eye contact –
it is the ground she must
keep her eyes on
(as if searching for lost
'worth' that has been shattered).
> *if anyone would just tell her*
> *what her crime was.*

the sad reality of this world
is that
it forces people into depression,
and then blames them
for being victim.
comparison fills the air
with toxicity,
expectations burden the heart
unnecessarily.
there is a rush
when time is one paced.
destinations are being chased,
when they aren't even moving.

> *(no wonder there are more people*
> *living in pieces, than there are in*
> *peace)*

do not sentence yourself
to death
for a culture,
that does not
understand your emotions.
this is the same culture
that weds girls
(in the shadows)
to men that can afford them,
and see men as earners
before humans with emotions.
if needs be *crawl*,
graze your knees trying,
and trying again,
but don't let culture
take another victim.
>*don't sentence yourself to death,*
>*for being human.*

the recurring cycle of anxiety
promises to worry your smile,
and quiver your laugh.
as if,
it is written to law
that happiness
(even momentarily)
must be followed by sadness.
as if,
happiness is temporary,
and sadness is not.
as if,
now that one problem is gone,
the next is waiting to come.
yet, the reality sits far
from this perception –
the sun and moon arrive,
as they depart,
differently in different seasons –
(it is not questioned).
> *the moments of life follow a similar*
> *pattern, it depends on one's*
> *perception.*

there are those who
remember the seed,
and those who
admire the rose.
there are those
who see thorns
as a warning of harm,
and those who
perceive them
as promisers of protection.
a rose does not shrink to its seed,
because of a nonbeliever's disbelief.
you do not become who you were
just because people are unwilling
to accept your maturity.

(perception either makes one grateful,
or consistently displeased)

this world tends to confuse
numbness with
strength.
in strength, one still feels –
yet in numbness,
emotions are enslaved
(and silenced) –
they are not allowed to run
freely within one's veins.
there is a difference
(so crucial)
between numbness and strength –
a difference *(so grave)* between
withholding and blocking.

it is strange,
the laws of science.
the fire that destroys all living
is created with an element
of human need –
yet also,
the same fire
falls to ashes by that
which all living dies without.
it is as simple as saying –
    need combined with the wrong
    elements equate destruction.

life is a constant trade-off
between what is,
and what could have been –
between what you lost,
and what you gained.
it happens,
that you lose that,
which you thought was
impossible to lose –
as it also happens,
that you gain that
which you believed
did not exist.

> *(it will always be: what you have,*
> *what you had,*
> *and the what ifs of*
> *what could have been)*

if you wish to change
your situation,
your status,
or your perception,
never wait for society to
echo its encouragement,
or culture to cheer on
its willingness.
society struggles with change,
and culture clashes
(head on)
with acceptance.
change for the better
starts from you,
for you.

>*(this world doesn't listen*
>*to dialogue,*
>*it only believes the act)*

what is in excess
is undervalued.
what becomes an addiction
is dangerous for you.
comparison in its nature
evokes ungratefulness.
hatred in this world
goes hand in hand
with obsession.
> *(this world wouldn't tell you,*
> *it can only show you)*

suicide happens
when the strong are told
they are weak,
and the brave are told
they are cowardly.
it happens,
when bullies are brushed off
as *'just'* children,
and the victims
are made to endure.
it happens,
when the past is defined
as the present,
and injustice is marked
on a person's soul.
maybe if mental health
was not a cultural dilemma,
lives would be saved
instead of egos.
> *(the unfortunate phase of ego*
> *over sentiments)*

strength is not about being okay,
it is *knowing* you will be.
it is closing the gates of your heart
to stitch your wounds
with self-love –
not saying you don't mind the blood.
it is learning to walk in the dark,
and dance in the rain –
not closing up and saying
you'll wait.
strength is *knowing*
you will look yourself in the eye
in the mirror one day,
tracing old scars,
past the tales of the past,
and say
(as you mean)
   'you do not bother me.'

the world is overflowing,
but loneliness still exists.
people often know directions,
but not destinations.
while some flowers bloom,
others do whither.
this world is cold,
but warm –
with love but,
undeniably,
embedded with cruelty.
> *(an imbalanced world where we*
> *foolishly expect stability)*

time does not stop
for your body to recover,
or your heart to heal,
or your soul to breathe.
time does not stop.
recovery must happen
in pain,
growth must happen,
in the rain,
and you must learn
to breathe
a little lighter
on the way.
time does not stop,
you can't hold moments
in place.

when they tell you,
you cannot achieve
the aspirations your heart
sings of,
do not bother your tongue,
in a feud.
nod to their arrogance,
and smile at your faith.
the seeds of success grow
in silence,
and feed on the egos
of those who do not believe.

stargazing under the sun

a note for

her

Monday 27th February 2017 –
may your soul rest in peace, always.

you broke mirrors,
trying to recreate yourself
pointing to the scars on your skin,
while you flattered the beauty
of every other soul
(no wonder you always saw yourself
as less).
you would tug the strings of your heart
with the past,
while you caressed every other heart
with the possibilities of their future
(no wonder you thought
there was nothing for you left).
you said to me then,
your presence wouldn't be missed
(no wonder everything has fallen out
of place since then).

> if only you knew the worth of your
> soul *(conversations I left for a next*
> *time that never came)*

flatline,
I heard it too.
it wasn't just you,
I heard it from my stability
too.
how ironic,
I'd lost my balance on a flat
rhythm,
just as your silence
started a commotion.
ironic,
how every heart started
listening,
when yours stopped
singing.
ironic,
how realisation
and affection,
are only welcomed after loss.
      I wish you had put your heart
      before theirs *(conversations I left*
      for a next time that never came)

the ones you lov*ed*,
love you *now*.
the ones you miss*ed*,
miss you *now*.
the ones you cri*ed* for
cry for you *now*.
it seems –
your closed eyes broke
their ego,
like your tearful ones
never did.
your expressionless face
brought them to their knees,
like your distressed one
never did.
I wonder if it matters –
the world knows
how to treat you *now*.
it echoes an apology
in the winds
and awaits your acceptance.
I wonder if it matters –
you've left its territory *now*.
        in response to the letters
they'll never receive (*conversations I left*
for a next time that never came)

there was a *beauty* of you
the passed the thin of your skin.
it made the air a little
lighter,
and made the birds sing
a little louder.
there was an *aura* about you,
the made the roses dance
with the winds,
and made the stars shine brighter.
there was so much to you –
so much,
that even the moon
unravelled itself
from the clouds,
to smile at you.

      if only you saw yourself the way I did
      (conversations I left for a next time
      that never came)

I hope you sit with the stars,
you were once searching for.
I hope you met the sun,
that you would reach out to.
I hope you found the peace,
this world failed to give you.
my promises are yours to keep,
I know you probably see.
this isn't goodbye,
this is till next time.
I will stargaze under the sun,
(for you)
till then.
                    sincerely your human diary.